CHANGE
YOUR
PERSPECTIVE

CHARLOTTE CAIN

This is a work of non-fiction. The events and scenarios in this book have been set down to the best of the author's ability, although some names and details have been changed to protect the privacy of individuals.

Scripture taken from the New King James Version®.

First Edition: April 2021

Book Cover & Interior design: Sam Rog

Editor: Kimberly Rose

ISBN 978-1-7371081-0-8

eBook ISBN 978-1-7371081-1-5

www.changeperspectivebook.com

Table of Contents

Chapters

Dedication

This book is dedicated to those who have experienced hurt, and it's still infringing pain in your life. My prayer is that this book will be an avenue to help you break free of the bondages and live a purpose-driven life.

Acknowledgements

To my precious gems (my children). I'm so grateful God
blessed me with you! You have inspired and taught me
so much about being a mother, friend and changing my
perspective too. The challenges we've faced made us
stronger and prepared us for our life journeys. "Momma
always got you!" God got us covered! Love you all to life!

To my parents, Thank you for teaching me about God,
loving, guiding, and supporting me. For loving and caring
for my children too. I'm grateful for both of you. I wouldn't
be who I am if it wasn't for you two! Greatness is y'all
destiny! I've got y'all too!   Love you both to life!

To my sisters, I'm grateful for y'all and the support and
encouragement you gave my children and I. The challenges
we've weathered only make us stronger. I've learned a lot
from both of you and am excited to see God do great things
in your lives. Love you all to life!

To my nieces and nephews (babies included), I'm grateful
for you all—the love you all give and the support. Keep
striving for greatness because it's in your destiny. Excited to

see God do great things in all of your lives. Love you all to life!

To my cousins, thank you for the support and encouragement needed at times I wanted to give up. The focus check-in were such a blessing! Forever grateful for you all! Love all of you to life!

To my Godmother, I thank God for your encouragement and support. Your wisdom and your understanding. Greatness is your destiny. I've got you too! Love you to life!

To my sisters in Christ! My squad, I'm so grateful for you all. The storms we've weathered and prayed through. Thank you all for being there for my children and I. I truly appreciate each of you. I'm so excited to see God do amazing things in your lives. Love you all to life!

To my future husband, covering you in prayer as God prepares our aligned destiny. Great things are in your future, King! I'm so grateful for you! Gods got US covered! Continue to grow and flow in God! Love you to life!

"Your Queen"

Introduction

This book conveys experiences from my life and others. Through the life experiences, I pray that something will resonate within you to give you the strength and encouragement you need to take a "Real" look at your life and recognize areas that could be better if you look at them from a different perspective. People often look at their situations through anger or fear due to offenses that may have been intentional or unintentional choices of others' behaviors. However, in this book, you're going to learn to look at life from a different lens allowing you to live a life that is less stressed, fearful, or hurtful. As you move forward, you will see where people are in their journey of life. Hence, trying to compare themselves to another's life is impossible because what God has placed in each person is uniquely designed for each individual. It's OK to admire others but not to the point of trying to emulate them or believe that they have what you're missing. This book will help you to analyze unhealthy relationships that you may need to let go of, make marriages stronger and help one heal from the broken areas of their life. This can be achieved as you move forward by growing through the healing process, being healthy, whole, and loving life in a new way. Without a doubt, this remarkable book is impactful. It will have you engaged as if you're listening to a close friend share wisdom, fresh perspective, and significant gems that you absorb to implement and change your life for the better. Get ready to take a deeper look into the gifts, skills, and purpose that you were given so that you can tap into those like never before. This will allow you to step out of the hangups that have kept you stagnant, the unhealthy thought processes, behaviors, doubting yourself, and looking for validation in the wrong places. This is why it's so important to take your eyes off of others and keep them on God, who will guide you through this process of changing your perspective so that you can change your life.

I am not a psychiatrist, but one that has experienced traumatic life situations. I realized through therapy, my walk with God, along with the major self-work, that I needed to fix my thought process if I ever wanted to experience and live the life that I was created to live.

Chapter 1

Overcome the Battle in your Mind

To accomplish anything in your life, you first have to overcome the battle in your mind. The space between your ears is crucial to how you function in life. What is your outlook on life? How do you think? The answer to these questions determines how far you will go. Do you look at life optimistically or negatively? Do you look at everything with a negative tone or always anticipating some plot to undermine what you're trying to do? Did you know that you'll receive those life scenarios if you give much energy to those thought processes? If that's what you're focusing on, you will receive that which you desire. I know you're ready to throw this book thinking, "You sound crazy! I don't desire those things. I've seen things and don't trust people, and that is why I'm cautious." There's nothing wrong with being cautious. We're supposed to use wisdom and discernment, but you're limiting yourself by always anticipating plots or schemes against yourself. Ask yourself this question and be honest. How often do you sit back and contemplate what person or situation is plotting against you? Are you comparing yourself to another? Ask three of your closest friends if you talk a lot, as if you're anticipating the other shoe about to drop, plots of getting over on you, or someone trying to put a monkey wrench in what you're doing. The only way this will work is if you're honest and candidly having this conversation and receptive to the feedback that they provide. Now, this has to come from friends or family who don't have an issue telling you the truth in love. If they say you appear to look at things with an extra skeptical eye, that is clearly an indicator that you have to overcome some battles in your mind. Your trust may have been challenged or shattered at some point in your life and you've lived your life not trusting people because of that. There's absolutely nothing wrong with paying attention to people because they get to show you who they are as you're getting to know them. But if you're consistently trying to test the person to see how trustworthy they are, if they're going to hurt or abandon you, then it's down to your mindset and not the other person. Somehow you've allowed what was done to you to color and control the relationships you're in and will be moving forward if you don't overcome this. Know that it's not another person's job to heal you or fill the void of unhealed areas in your childhood, adolescence, or even adult life. That is an unrealistic expectation and they aren't God! You have to decide to deal with the brokenness by

2

doing the work by yourself or with a therapist. Placing that responsibility on a spouse, friend, parent, or family member is not fair nor logical. They can support you, but they can't be the person to fix it for you because that's totally up to you! You have to make peace with the situation and people who've caused the distrust or negative emotion. This doesn't excuse what they did or give them a pass. Acknowledge your feelings about the circumstance, then make a conscious decision to choose to forgive. Doing so gives you the peace of mind that you truly deserve, which no longer allows the situation to have power over you now or in your future. Please don't seek out unhealthy interactions with that person. If you can have a healthy, non-violent, and loving discussion, do so with another party present, such as a therapist via phone. If you cannot, it's perfectly fine to make peace within yourself.

In most cases, it's best to do the Release Letter method, especially if you're unsure how you or the person will interact. To make peace within, write a letter to them of all that occurred and how it made you feel. Above all, acknowledge your area of responsibility and how it possibly made them feel too. Apologize for the role you played and end the letter by making peace with the entire situation. Fold the letter, and place it in an envelope, and be present in how you're feeling. Take a deep breath and repeat this prayer, *"I choose to let go (name all that occurred and how it made you feel). I choose to forgive, not by my feelings, but by choice, as this will no longer have power over my present or future life. All things from this situation have been uprooted. The reign it has over my life ends today. I renounce these things and thank God for delivering me out of the bondage that those things have held me in. I'm not defined by what I went through but by the life that I choose to live. I forgive (name the offender and/or yourself). I walk in freedom from this moment forward. My feelings will get in line with my confession because I'm free in the name of Jesus, Amen, Amen, and Amen!"* List the date and time that you wrote this letter. You can either burn the letter as your release or keep it in a safe place to reflect on what God freed you from. Receive that healing! Now, walk in that healing of letting go and letting God give you closure about the situation. Whether you speak to the person or not. Sometimes even speaking to the person of offense doesn't bring about the closure you'd hope for, which is why looking to God is vital. However, if you can talk with them, agree to discuss with a mindset of resolve. Let me explain what I mean by this? Be careful not to use the discussion as a "Blame Game" session. Ensure that you're ready to own your part of the responsibility in the breakdown of the relationship. Be open to hear what the other person has to say without being offended. Be mindful that as this conversation is occurring,

its purpose is for the revealing and healing process. This is not the time to get them to see things your way but to express what happened and how it made both of you feel. You can agree to disagree if needed, apologize, let go, and move forward peacefully. Everyone is not on the same page spiritually, mentally, and emotionally. This is not to belittle anyone but to give you an understanding that everyone is in their own lane and flowing at their own pace. When you choose to accept people where they are, it relieves you from the unnecessary stress of trying to get them to fit the mold of where you feel they should be. Know that God doesn't force His will upon us. So, don't try to push yours upon others. The purpose of the discussion is to acknowledge, release, let go, and find peace to move on without allowing the circumstance to keep you in bondage. You deserve a healthy life and relationships now and moving forward. Again, you could have a simple phone conversation with a therapist or trusted third party present, **ONLY** if it's a **non-violent** situation. If the situation is out of control (unforgiveness, anger, bitterness, or the person is abusive, or any negative interactions, then **do not engage!**) If no negative factors apply. When the discussion is over, choose to forgive and hang up peaceably. Once you're off the phone, make a conscious decision to forgive. If your feelings are not in a forgiving place, acknowledge what you're feeling, but don't stay there. Take a deep breath and repeat this prayer: *"I choose to let go of (name all that occurred and how it makes you feel). I choose to forgive not by my feelings but by choice, as this will no longer have power over my present or future life. All things from this situation have been uprooted. The reign it has over my life ends today. I renounce these things and thank God for delivering me out of the bondage that those things have held me in. I'm not defined by what I went through but by the life that I choose to live. I forgive (name the offender and/or yourself). I walk in freedom from this moment forward. My feelings will get in line with my confession because I'm free in the name of Jesus, Amen, Amen, and Amen!"* Receive the healing! In the journal section of this book, write the date and time this took place, and thank God that it is now behind you. Now, move forward peacefully. If you have ever been victimized, my suggestion is to reach out to a therapist to help you walk through this process of healing.

However, I've seen people forgive by using the release letter method regarding their situation as their relief to get things out of their system completely. They chose to come from a place of victor and no longer a victim. Here's Janice's process. It's still a daily routine for Janice, but she does the following to maintain her progress; studying and reading the Bible, joining a small Bible study group at her church, reading self-help books, saying affirmations, and monitoring what she's feeding her mind and spirit. Above all, she adjusted her circle of friends. She understands that entertaining negative influences and negative thoughts could set her back into a negative space. Eventually taking her backward emotionally, which she's experienced. This is why she's really disciplined in maintaining her steps even though things got easier. She's forgiven and made peace within herself. Janice started engaging in some things she'd put on hold since that negative situation took precedence over everything in her life. Now she's in school, and her living arrangements are better. She is active in her church and helps others get free by sharing her testimony of no longer allowing her past to plague her life. Making those daily steps has helped her come a very long way from where she started to complete healing.

I've also seen people hold onto hurt for far too long and how it negatively affects their life. How they interact with their family, friends, coworkers, relationships, and how it's affected their personal growth. They play the blame game very well. They are not happy with their lives. They attract other unhealed relationships since they have become accustomed to this way of thinking and living. If you try to tell them differently, they get easily offended, and if given real examples, they deflect to someone else because they don't want to deal with that area of their life. The past can be a holding place for people that haven't chosen to break free of its grasp, thereby causing them to knowingly or unknowingly be enslaved to it. They don't see that this perspective is choosing to live life through those past colored lenses. In the next chapter, let's take a closer look at more life experiences of people who need to overcome their minds' battles.

Chapter 2

Break Free of Mental Bondages

This chapter will allow you to step into some of the challenges people have faced and their methods to resolve them—Joey, who feels every woman will hurt him because his wife broke his heart. Now lives in broken relationships. He doesn't choose to connect to one woman but multiple women. His reason is fear that they will afflict pain, just as his wife did. He's constantly wondering what he lacked that caused the betrayal. So to protect his unhealed heart, he's chosen to stay clear of relationships. Whenever he starts to feel something for one woman, he sabotages it by engaging with another. Hurt people hurt others. His angst of opening his heart again to love has him fill the void with multiple women. He believes that if women enjoy his bedroom antics, he'll be in a good position to build himself up. For those moments of pleasure, he feels on top of the world, but after every ejaculation, reality hits home and he's back to feeling the way he did before. Knowing that his heart is in turmoil makes him feel like a wimp. Because he was always taught a man is supposed to be strong. Unfortunately, he was never taught how to handle the matters of his heart. Joey is lost and needs help but too prideful and stubborn to ask or talk to anyone about it. So he keeps sifting through life, trying to mend his aching heart with temporary thrills.

Next is Linda, who's sharp with her tongue. She's quick to let her boyfriend know who's the boss because of the relationship she saw her parents have before they divorced. Linda tries to control her boyfriend because she feels her mother was too lenient with her dad and shouldn't have allowed half the things he did in their marriage. So, she vowed never to be that woman, and due to fear, she's excessively controlling and treats her boyfriend as a child instead of her man. Her insecurities are being placed upon him, which bothers him at times. However, he still loves her so much that he's trying to prove that he's not her father and won't hurt nor abandon her as he did. Her behavior gets out of control, and he finally lets her know that he has booked a therapist. He did this because he loves her, and in order for them to have a healthy relationship, they both have to undergo healing. He's acknowledged his issues and clearly sees hers too. They went to therapy and started working on the negative experiences they've faced so they can heal their brokenness and move forward with a healthier relationship.

Let's look at Uncle Jeffrey, whose business collapsed ten years ago. He can't stand anyone talking about starting a business. He overheard his cousin ask a close friend of the family about the ups and downs of it. Uncle Jeffrey interjected and advised against it, not recognizing that his situation was only a setback. He could've revamped the business and came back stronger, but instead, he allowed the hurt, anger, shame, and fear to keep him from trying again. So, he spews negative fuel in the ears of all that will listen to the many reasons why they should continue to work a job instead of run their own business.

Here's Tasha, a single mother whose son is married, and because she has never healed from her previous marriage and issues with her father, she causes issues in her son's marriage. She's positioned him as her (so-called) man. This type of relationship is called covert incest when parents look to their child for emotional support otherwise given by another adult (usually a romantic partner). However, this connection with the child is not sexual. Trey is Tasha's son, and he is married to Janine. Janine has requested several times for Trey to establish healthy boundaries with his mother. Janine knows this kind of kinship is not normal and, after they attended counseling, the official name was revealed to be "Covert Incest." Being a young married couple in their early twenties.

Establishing who they are individually from their birth family is still a work in progress. They are both still naturally flowing with the programming of their upbringing, family traditions, behaviors, thought processes, and attitudes, to say the least. Being so young, married, with two children, and a new home was a lot to juggle. Not to mention the family dynamics that interfered countlessly. This situation revealed to Janine that it would be impossible to win her mother-in-law over because no matter what, she'd already decided whether she liked Janine or not. Unbeknownst to Tasha, her abundance of errand requests for Trey left him annoyed, drained, and procrastinate in doing any more for his mom. But Janine was the voice in his ear, nudging him to comply with her request. Tasha was a broken person hindering her son and his wife's relationship. Tasha often treated Janine as the other woman, which is the typical response from a parent that resonates with the Covert Incest mentality. Janine and Trey's therapist tried to help them understand that many relationships deal with these psychological issues when parents place their child in that role. Having that psychological viewpoint still took Janine some time to adjust. But analyzing Tasha's behavior from that perspective did help explain the weirdness Janine initially felt. It brought awareness that Tasha's issue with Janine wasn't personal but psychological. She hadn't reconciled her past. Trey and Janine's marriage eventually ended in divorce, and many factors played a role, and this was one of them. Trey wasn't ready to do the work necessary to change and establish the boundaries needed. What goes unchecked never gets healed. Trey never addressed his mother about the unhealthy relationship. Years later, after the divorce, Trey realized how important the boundaries were, yet still struggles with breaking free of the Emotional Incest whenever in Tasha's presence.

Let's look at this final scenario; Francine and Jermaine are married with two beautiful children, Shana and April. For several years, it was a family of four, and they were all set. However, one magical night led to their family being expanded to a family of five. Being the youngest of the two siblings, April didn't take too well to a new addition coming into their family. When baby Naomi was born, April felt resentment for she'd been the baby of the house for several years. As the girls grew older, April began to allow the resentment to turn into a rivalry. She'd always looked at Naomi as the culprit that stole her position as the family's baby. But little did she know that Naomi had no say in her time of arrival into the family. April, Shana, and Naomi had some good times. Naomi would watch her sisters dance to the record player, as it played "Boogie Shoes," "Purple Rain," and many more songs. However, with no warning, April would shift and pick on Naomi. When

Naomi would run to tell her mom, Francine dismissed things, stating to "ignore your sister and let it go," as some parents would. Naomi did just that, but the issue was April never let it go. Things would be great and groovy again, and then just like Dr. Jekyll and Mrs. Hyde, April would switch. April once told Naomi she was adopted. When April made that statement, Naomi now understood why she was being treated differently and why April's behavior was allowed. Naomi felt like she didn't belong in the family from her earliest memories and constantly escaped mentally to her imaginary friends and family that lived in the kitchen wall panel. There is where she found love, protection, and a sense of belonging. Naomi was angry because nothing was being done to fix the issue. She couldn't tell her mom because nothing would change. Telling her mother only brought about continued excuses that subconsciously taught her to suppress her feelings for the sake of her sister and later on in life, for others' sake. Being told she was adopted meant her own family didn't love her enough to keep her. Talk about feeling unloved and unwanted; that was Naomi's predicament. One day, while Naomi talked to her cousin, she learned that she wasn't adopted after all. That brought forth more confusion and questions for Naomi. Naomi loves April, and many times wondered what did she do, so wrong to be treated that way. Why did she and her sister have a love-hate relationship? That wasn't her relationship with Shana. Why was God allowing this to happen to her? Many nights, she wished she was a part of someone else's family? People can have good times, but when a flurry of negative things happens. It changes the thought process and your view on people and things if not addressed and handled. The Huxtables were Naomi's imaginary family, for they always addressed their issues, talked through things, and healed. But that wasn't the case in Naomi's home. As they got older, the rivalry escalated to a physical display of anger; No arguments, no heated discussion, just out of the blue slap to the head, earrings snatched out of ears, thumped in the temple, etc. Jermaine saw what was going on, and he would say something to April, but she would run to Francine, and there would be a heated argument between the parents. In an effort to keep peace in the home, Jermaine picked and chose his discussions. He shielded Naomi from the foolishness as best as he could. Jermaine began to keep Naomi with him as much as possible. He worked and drank a bit much at that time. Naomi realized this might have been one of his triggers for drinking. As this daddy and daughter bond grew, she learned how to maintain outside of the home, barbecue, work on cars and work on things in the house. She'd travel out of town with her dad too. Wherever you saw Jermaine, you would see Naomi. Naomi was daddy's little girl, and she would talk to her dad about his drinking. Finally, Jermaine went to Alcoholics Anonymous and overcame his addiction. Growing up, Naomi felt frustrated and unprotected by her mom. Being a victim of her sister's unhealed, unchecked resentment and anger as the middle child had Naomi fed up. However, Naomi has been doing the work to heal individually. She would always ask God to uproot the deep-rooted issues regarding her relationship with her sister, both consciously and subconsciously, and God did just that. She prayed and asked God to strip the hurt, resentment, frustration, and anger away. She asked Him to position her in a place to protect her heart but not close it entirely, for she genuinely loves her sister. She also asks God to protect her other relationships so what happened wouldn't color her lens towards other sisterhoods. Naomi asked God to heal her from suppressing her feelings for the sake of others, and she's still getting better day by day. She listed all of the occurrences and even prayed for those that may occur in the future. She's praying for her sister so they can have a beautifully healthy, healed, and whole relationship someday. Naomi followed the same strategy regarding her hurt and resentment with her mother. Naomi loves her mother dearly and saw what many mothers see; which child is stronger and needs them the most. At first, it didn't make sense how she neglected to handle things the right way. Although taking a glimpse into where a parent is mentally and emotionally at a specific time in their life helps provide a greater understanding. Choosing to forgive is very powerful and liberating! Naomi decided to look at things differently because she looked through a victim's lens for a long time. Naomi understands that most parents typically operate from what they know to do or have seen emotionally, mentally, and spiritually. She extends grace to her mother because no one is perfect. She chooses to grow and heal to prevent this from turning generational. As she thrives in her healing process, significant knowledge is revealed about her past and present relationships. Naomi and April still have some good times, but until April is determined to heal and do the work, Naomi will continue to love her from a distance.

In life, protecting your peace is key. You can't force people to deal or heal just because you choose to. But it's your responsibility to heal and move forward in love. Dealing with family issues is critical Getting the help needed and starting the healing process is necessary because what doesn't get fixed continues to spill over into one's present and future if not properly addressed. Although some people use their hurt and pain as a crutch, others are unsure about the process as they've been accustomed to this behavior and mentality for so long that they are scared of whom they will become if they change. Instead of choosing to mend, fear causes people to stay stuck and not deal with the issues that need to be addressed. Many families can step into the reconciling process by getting help or doing the internal work. Concentrate on the issues. Don't let things go unresolved. Eldridge Cleaver said it best, "Be a part of the solution, not a part of the problem." The process causes you to look at the issues, deal with yourself, ask God to uproot those things that keep you bound consciously and subconsciously. Choose to get to the root of the issue and not just the fruit. You have to overcome the battles in your mind. You have to push past the fear, anxiety, and negative thoughts that will try to keep you from seeking help from a therapist, friend, pastor, or counselor. How you think and how you feel plays a major role in how you live. You must be in tune with your thoughts.

There's an acronym F.E.A.R., and according to Google, it stands for False Evidence Appearing Real. There's no true immediate danger or threat of loss, and that F.E.A.R. is merely an illusion. Then there's anxiety which is nothing but repeatedly re-experiencing failure in advance, which is a 'waste' according to Seth Godin, Copyblogger. Still, those very two things keep many people stagnant and stuck in the fear pattern of their minds replaying negative scenarios that are merely the enemy's tactics to keep people from healing completely. Are you casting those negative thoughts down and replacing them with positive thoughts. Every time you think negative thoughts, it creates neural pathways in your brain, and the more you reflect (replay the negative situation in your mind), the darker the neural pathways are formed to cover a large portion of your brain. However, you have the ability to reconstruct the paths in your brain by consciously, consistently selecting to replace them with good and positive thoughts. Take every thought captive as stated in 2 Corinthians 10:5 NKJV. This verse is a call to action. When you cast down negative thoughts and think about good things, you change and create new neural pathways in your brain that affect your body's general health. How you think affects your mood, feeling, health, etc. Your brain affects every area of your body, so watch what you're feeding it. Are you watching drama shows, the news, or horror films all the time? Engaging in such activities can cause stress or can raise your blood pressure. If you think I'm joking, watch three or more of those shows (back to back) and see what your heart rate will state on your smartwatch. Scrolling through social media changes your mood consistently, though it depends on the post. You'll go from happy to sad, to laughing then crying, up and down constantly. We take our bodies through so many emotional and mental feelings that we have to be more mindful of what we're feeding our mind, body, and spirit! Pay more attention to what you tune into. Limit how often you watch TV and other visual devices. Healthy balance and self-discipline are truly needed when it comes to your diets, mental, emotional, spiritual, physical, and financial health. How you handle these areas affects your quality and quantity of life. Choose positive vibes and good energy. Protect your peace by being selective of those that can access that space in your life.

Overcoming the battle in your mind takes moving past your fears, anxiety, and negative thought processes. Making a choice to release all of the pain from difficult situations and forgive while making peace with it. Make a conscious decision to trust the healing process and replace negative thoughts with positive ones. Put steps in place to monitor what you're feeding your mind, body, and spirit. What you feed your mind affects your soul. What you think affects you as a whole, especially as the brain sends signals to every area of your body. Now that you know how to overcome the battles in your mind. It would behoove you to change your attitude to begin to think about things differently.

Let your mindset elevate you to higher levels in life so that you can live life purposefully. The scenarios presented were to give you life examples to help you, your family, and friends self-reflect and see if there are areas you're ignoring. Areas where you may need help and are afraid to ask. Seeing these, I pray it helps you realize the effect thought processes, behaviors, and actions can have if they are left unaddressed or unhealed. On this journey of life, we all go through our ups and downs. No one's perfect. However, electing to recover from the things we go through is critical because it affects our lives, the lives of our spouse, children, grandchildren, and every other person we encounter. Seek the help. Commit to going through the healing process to change not only yours but your family's life and the world around you.

Chapter 3

Change Your Attitude

The next step in changing your perspective is changing your attitude. You've gotten over the fear and come out of staying stuck in your past, willing to establish a new normal for your life. However, your attitude needs to adjust. Attitude is your emotions, beliefs, and feelings about someone, something, or situations. They can result from what you've gone through, but usually, it's from what you've seen or been taught growing up. Attitudes will affect your behavior. This is why it's so important to work on your attitude.

This book will talk about 5 types of attitudes; Positive, Negative, Neutral, Sikken, and Godly. Positive attitudes reflect a person that typically focuses on the good in any circumstance. When difficult situations occur or they make a mistake, they find the good in it and look at the opportunity to grow and evolve. Positive people are flexible, take responsibility, and are optimistic. People with Negative attitudes focus on the bad in circumstances. They complain, blame others, and make no effort to change. Their thought process is all that matters, and listening to other's opinions would be a major debate as they'd bring all the negative connotations in an attempt to sway you to their negative thought process. People with negative attitudes are angry, doubters, and jealous, to name a few examples. Those with Neutral Attitudes are indifferent or complacent. They don't focus enough on certain people or circumstances. They are typically looking for someone else to solve issues as they don't want to be the problem solver. They are comfortable being in the complacent lane. The Sikken Attitudes are considered the most aggressive of attitudes as this person will destroy any thought of positivity. What goes on with them is deeply rooted, and it's extremely challenging to get them to change their thought process. Intense therapy is needed for this individual. Finally, you have the Godly attitude that reflects a person of great faith and humility. People with a Godly attitude look at life with hope, even in the darkest events or circumstances. They have hope and come from a place of love. They are humble in their demeanor, knowing that if it wasn't for the grace of God, they would be lost and their lives are far from perfect. They are always grateful to God that they don't look like what they've been through. They encourage others along their journeys. They live a humble life filled with faith, working towards their lives' high calling. After learning about the different types of attitudes, what category would you fall in? Do you need to change your attitude? An attitude adjustment is necessary if you keep looking at life negatively, blaming others, and removing all hope of positivity. Now it's time to go deeper in changing your attitude. Your disposition about the situation needs to change. Walking in freedom takes work. You don't want to go backward. You've developed your attitude over the years because of the environment you grew up in, or you may have altered your attitude now that you're older and engaging new people whose influences have shifted your attitude. Nevertheless, it's time to look at life differently. Do you recall the prayer of choosing to forgive not by your feelings but by choice in the first chapter? It's time to put in the work to align your feelings with that prayer. Did you know that your feelings are fleeting, and they don't have intelligence? Saying you forgive but still exhibiting a nasty attitude is not the way to live completely free. The situation that happened to you shouldn't define you for the rest of your life. Choosing to forgive is powerful and liberating. For those that have neutral and negative attitudes, you have to submit to the will of God! Yes, the situation that occurred was messed up. That person was wrong for what they did. But remember, you chose to forgive. It doesn't mean that you have to be the best of friends. But you're choosing to do the work to feel different. Feelings have no intellect, so you must take control of how you feel. A negative person needs to choose to let go and operate from a frequency of love and understanding. You're electing to be free when you positively think of the situation moving forward. It doesn't put you in a tailspin, and you're not in your feelings. You noticed what it was but decided to be of a strong mentality as this; Even though they hurt you when you hear their name, see them, or hear their voice, you're not cringing anymore. You don't have unforgiveness nor a stinking disposition about them. It's time to think and feel about them from a victor mentality and not a victim anymore. What happened to you does not characterize you, nor can it keep you from the great life God has called you to live, just as you used countless times to put negative energy into the universe. You can apply that same energy and allow it to work productively for you by choosing to forgive and make peace with the entire situation or person to ensure that you are no longer giving energy to your past, which doesn't deserve it. Channel that same energy for good thoughts, good feelings, new visualizations, and the complete change of your attitude about the situation and/or the person.

Chapter 4

See Things Differently

To see things differently, you have to look at situations from a different point of view. For example, when a coworker is short-tempered with you and finds issues with your report, look at it differently. The coworker could be going through some family or relational issues. Instead of going into defense mode, ask them to advise what needs to be fixed with the report and if everything is OK. They may or may not confide in you, but the way you look at it helps deescalate the situation. With this, your coworker is aware that you're attentive and that they need to pull it together, calm down, or confide in you to get it off their chest. Now, if the discrepancies found in your report are legitimate, then it was good that your coworker brought them to your attention. However, your response lets them know their approach in addressing this was less than kind. Learning not to be offended every time you don't like what is being said helps lower your stress and keeps you from overreacting. Many things in life can have your blood pressure up or have you stressed out of your mind. But learn to take a deep breath and look at life from a place of love. People have issues. Not everyone chooses to get help or is willing to admit that they need help. Some people have wallowed in their pain and anger for so long; it's attached itself as a legitimate personality trait. The only reason it's still there is that the person has not done the work needed to be free from those negative thoughts, attitudes, and behaviors. Some people are scared that if they go through the healing process, they won't know the person that'll emerge on the other side of it—others like the attention, the excuses made for their behavior. Having a different outlook takes intentionality to change one's perspective. You need to make a conscious decision for this turnaround and implement it daily. Choose not to be easily offended. It's time to get thicker skin. Wounded people act ugly, gossip, hurt others, manipulate, think and speak negatively, those are different variations of brokenness inside them. Therefore you must always come from a place of love. It's your responsibility how you respond to others. This step takes some patience, grace, and time. If a person says or does something hurtful naturally, people get upset. Just because that person acted in a nasty way, don't repay them. Being kind, calm, and cool actually reaps coals on their head. When you don't allow the embarrassment, lies, or hurts to cause you to step outside your cool zone. You cause them to be in that boat all by themselves. Listen, we are all humans. We all have our moments, and when you do, because it happens, don't feel that you've blown it. Dust yourself off. Analyze what set you off and incorporate that into the strategy to work on with the affirmations and visualization of seeing yourself responding differently moving forward. Habitual practice turns into a natural flow. Learning to see things differently elevated my thought process! No longer was I on the constant emotional roller coasters when someone did something I didn't like. I removed their control from my life. By regulating how I felt while people tried to bait me, I learned the tactics and strategies. They never change. They only alter from person to person in their delivery. It's also vital to pray, especially about certain conversations or interactions, before engaging because some tactics are so subtle. Remember, the tactics always target things you are most passionate about and are your weaknesses. They could be desires, failures, unhealed areas, or the healing process you're walking through. The enemy doesn't want you to graduate to see things differently. Instead, he wants you to remain in bondage, being a victim with resentment, anger, hurt, guilt, shame, bitterness, failure, and unforgiveness. If he can keep you flowing in that capacity, then he can keep you from completely healing and living a life with purpose. Hearing that should bring such an awakening that you choose not to stay in a daze of repetitive negative thoughts or emotions. But to wake up and live because there's so much more that God has in store for you. Know that He can use the things you've been through to make your life better than it ever was before, allow Him to alter your outlook to His view. That entails releasing your will for His will, your way for His way, and your thoughts for His thoughts. Then let go and keep moving towards the mark of your goal.

The next step is going deeper in protecting your peace. Setting healthy boundaries is key, and agreeing not to hit below the belt when you're in an argument is imperative. Whether it's your spouse, family, friends, roommates, business partners, or partners, following those guidelines contributes to a healthy relationship. Handle things by talking it out. If you need time to think, set an agreed-upon time, so the heated conversations don't escalate. When the two of you regroup to talk, come from a place of understanding, love, and resolution. Bear in mind; you're not truly listening if you're only listening to refute their statement. Which means you're only trying to be heard. When you don't listen, nothing gets resolved! It's not about winning the argument but sincerely listening with your heart. Please take in what the other is saying and paraphrase it back to them to ensure you're comprehending exactly what they are trying to convey. The object of the conversation is resolution. Be what you want in return. Be mindful that everyone is on different quests. Extend the same grace that you'd like someone to extend to you. This doesn't mean you have to be a doormat. It means, be understanding yet wise. Here's another scenario to further drive this point home.

Alex and Carmen are in an exclusive, committed relationship; however, Alex was lying and cheating on Carmen. He'd often blame Carmen for his inconsistency and inability to be honest and faithful. The last straw was Alex moving Nina into his house unbeknownst to Carmen. Carmen was focused on her children's projects with school and wasn't visiting as often this particular week but still communicated via phone with Alex daily. He told Carmen he's finally going to bed early to ensure he's well-rested for his morning shift. Carmen understood. As he'd always say, he was going to bed early but never stuck to it. The children's school projects were completed early. Carmen chose to surprise Alex as she'd often do in the past by bringing over a cooked meal for them to eat dinner together. Alex was shocked that she showed up and was acting weird in his house. She started to leave because of the lame excuses he gave. But it didn't sit right with her. She told him she needed to use the bathroom. In the bathroom, she could hear him scurrying around the house. She noticed female items in the corner of the tub that wasn't hers. When she came out of the bathroom, she went directly to his bedroom; she saw additional items that belonged to another woman. Carmen angrily grabbed her belongings out of the dresser drawer and went to the kitchen to grab the food she'd brought over. Alex wrestled with her to get the container of food out of her hand, with arms mostly filled with her belongings that weren't hard to do. She scuffled with him to get her container of food back. He cradled the food container and tussled with her to the door, giving her the stiff arm as a football player would to block and keep another from getting the ball. She was close to the door and out of frustration, concluded that this would be the last meal he'd receive from her. She went to her car and left. Alex selfishly kept the food Carmen brought over. As usual, Alex made excuses and didn't take responsibility for his actions. He tried to play the guilt trip and blamed Carmen for popping up without notice. But in a two-year relationship, this was Carmen's ordinary sweet gesture. He finally took accountability, stating he was ashamed of his behavior. Needless to say, Carmen bumped her head a few more months, operating out of her feelings before she learned to no longer be his doormat, for his behavior got worse! Alex's behavior clearly shows unresolved and unhealed issues from his life. He would give good advice but never applied it to his own life. He's broken and in denial of needing help. He believes that people can't handle the truth, and this is why he lies. Extend grace, come from a place of understanding and love but use wisdom not to be another person's doormat. Carmen was dealing with self-esteem issues but finally took steps to start her healing process using the release letter method. She's able to love again and not have the fear that the next guy will hurt her as Alex did. Her changed perspective resolved her self-esteem issue and helped her move on without allowing what happened to cloud her view on relationships, men, or life. You can love people, be understanding but use wisdom to no longer allow certain people access to your life. Protect your peace.

The final step is to send out positive vibrations. Start your days studying the Bible, praying, praising, and worshipping. Listen to uplifting songs and watch cheerful and funny TV shows. Also, engage in upbeat, positive conversations, healthy reading material, and books with a lot of zeal. Positive vibrations attract just as negative ones do, so speak positive affirmations. You can enjoy a person's company, but if they keep up drama or are disrespectful. Love them where they are but know and establish your healthy boundaries. Everyone doesn't get access to the inner you: Your home, spouse, children, or family; that's your safe space. It has nothing to do with trust. But everything to do with positive vibrations and the leading of God. Jesus had twelve disciples, and out of the twelve, you'd hear about a few in particular. Jesus didn't take all of them to his most vulnerable places. Keep that in mind! Your life is extraordinary, and when you consider yourself special, everyone doesn't get full access to you. Monitor what you listen to because positive vibrations are pivotal. When you're flowing with a healthy mindset, elevation comes naturally.

Chapter 5

Mindset Determines Your Altitude

One's mindset determines their altitude in life. The Bible says in Proverbs 23:7NKJV, "For as he thinks in his heart, so is he." This scripture says that the thoughts and desires of one's heart shape who one is. Your thoughts shape your actions. Your actions show what you'll do. You will do and become what you think. Think about it, if you view everything negatively, how can you elevate to a positive level? All you'd see are negative thoughts instead of positives. Negativity pulls you down; it doesn't elevate. When people talk about negative situations in their lives, they give an enormous amount of energy to those circumstances through their words, feelings, and thoughts. Keep in mind that if you don't neutralize them, you're well on your way to receiving those situations if they are not presently occurring in your life. Always having untrustworthy and negative thoughts of someone trying to get over on you. That's countless minutes of negative energy that you're sowing. By entertaining those thoughts, you're telling the universe that's what you want to reap. Whether you comprehend it or not, that is what you're subconsciously attracting to your life. Have you heard of "The Laws of Attraction?" This philosophy stems from repetitive thoughts, feelings, emotions, and energy that a person focuses upon. Suppose you don't want the negative things that you've taken countless time giving power to. Then you'll need to neutralize those thoughts, words, and energy. To counteract the negative things you've focused on, say this prayer; *"Lord, I choose to cancel (list the things you've said, thought about, and given energy to) that I've spoken, thought about, and given energy to and replace them with (list positive thoughts you actually want in your life.) I receive the positive things that I've said, and I thank you for turning things around in the mighty name of Jesus I Pray Amen, Amen, and Amen.* Then by faith, receive the positive thoughts you've prayed for. Now, invest the time to think, speak, and give energy to the positive thoughts you want to manifest in your life. You're worth it! Write and repeat the positive things you desire at least five times throughout the day with intense emotion. Next, start visualizing by closing your eyes, being clear, and think of how you'd feel and express it, then take in that good energy of what you've prayed for, seeing it play out on the screen of your mind! I've fallen asleep at home plenty of times doing this method. Take that same energy you'd use negatively and allow it to productively work for you by choosing to forgive and make peace with the situation to ensure that you are no longer giving energy to your past. Your past doesn't define you. Know that you are a victor. Forgive the person because if you don't, what occurred will continue to weigh you down mentally, emotionally, and spiritually, affecting you physically. It will keep you stuck replaying what took place over and over again on the screen of your mind. You deserve to be free of what happened to you. Free of how it has tried to stunt your growth and the purpose God has placed on your life. When things happen, sometimes its purpose is to derail the plan for your life. I'm here to let you know that a detour doesn't mean that you can't reroute and get back on the path to your destiny. You deserve a life that is healthy, healed, and whole.

This scenario gives more insight into how one's mindset determines your altitude. When Dennis and Sheila lost their marital home, Shelia searched for a new residence for the children and herself, but nothing she saw was suitable for them. The children and Sheila moved back home with Sheilas' parents. This was not a gratifying move, but it was a blessing. Losing their home and separating (while being indecisive on making their marriage work), there were many factors to weigh. Sheila rehearsed all the negative things that were going on in her life. The frustrations she felt and faced.

She gave energy, thoughts, and spoken words to countless hours and days of the negative things she was dealing with. She didn't speak life; she said what she felt. That is the biggest trick of the enemy. When you're frustrated and upset, instead of speaking life, you murmur and complain, thinking about the situation replaying the scenario's in your mind. Then you talk to one person to see if you were wrong. You talk to another and another before you finally make an appointment with a therapist or your pastor. By the time you're done, you've spoken about the situation seventy times over. Guess what? Shelia received more negative issues to talk about. The couple decided to work on their marriage again. Shelia was fully committed, but Dennis's actions showed fickleness. He wanted the benefits of being married without actually exhibiting the commitment. The children witnessed their parents' behavior. Their father made excuses why he couldn't spend time or provide for them. Their mother was fussing in her bedroom and the kitchen. Sometimes she'd go to her car so they wouldn't hear her lament. Living with her parents trying to maintain sanity amid all these changes was difficult to handle. Sheila kept murmuring and complaining to all who'd listen. Sheila initiated therapy to help have an objective third party, including their pastors and other Christian counselors. Dennis would attend and give his input on things. However, he'd walk right out of sessions and go back to whatever it was he wanted to do. Sheila started having separate sessions because she needed to heal. The limbo game was getting old, but she needed the strength to decide because it appeared Dennis wasn't going to heal at all. Sheila read self-help and prayer books to help her grow as a woman. She read and studied the Bible and taught their children as well. They began to pray for their new home, and Sheila began to describe it as her visions revealed it. The children would chime in and pray for their new home with specific bold prayers! Because of being laid off, Sheila added financial struggle into her prayers. However, she acquired a new job, but it didn't pay as lucrative as the previous position did. God answered their prayer. They received their new home, and it was 'All' because of God! Sheila had just enough money to buy the children's beds and beddings. She slept on her bedroom floor in a sleeping bag with totes that held her clothing. She'd acquired her own place. It felt great! The financial struggle continued along with the co-parenting issues. But Sheila persevered. When bouncing back from a setback, you usually don't feel like it because you're in the thick of it. Be aware that God is developing you and turning things around for your highest good in the wilderness. God uses what you're going through to lift you by elevating your mindset and stripping you of all the things that weren't good for you. Such as things that no longer serve your life's purpose. He's stretching you to see if He can trust you with little before he blesses you with much. He's pruning you, snipping away the unhealthy parts so the healthy aspects of your life can flourish and no longer be stifled in growth. He's preparing you for the next phase of your life. Your life hasn't ended. It's just beginning. You're learning who you are in Him without the distraction. When you're quiet, lying on your bedroom floor in the middle of the night and everyone is asleep. It's just you with your thoughts. Will you praise Him? Will you thank Him even if you don't have everything you want? Will you thank Him even when situations are still in limbo and you don't know which way it's going to turn? Will you thank Him even if you don't see how you're going to put food on the table and clothes on your children's back? When you're trying to keep the lights and gas on. Will you thank and trust Him? Sheila started to let go of Dennis! She asked God to put a guard over her mouth. Help her not be harsh because he was a bitter person neglecting their children out of spite. He didn't realize that he was punishing his flesh and blood. Damaged people damage others, whether consciously or subconsciously, and everyone's hurt level is different. Dennis attended the therapy sessions but his actions and thought process showed he wasn't doing the needed work. Therapists can only do so much. It's up to the person to choose to heal, think healthily, operate from a place of love, extend grace and forgive, take accountability, and elect to do what's morally right! After three years of limbo, Sheila finally had enough. She was willing, but Dennis wasn't. In truth, nothing gets resolved if the two are not consistently on the same page working toward the same goal. When Sheila let go and decided to no longer give Dennis control over her life, it was liberating. No one can control you unless you allow what they do to disturb you. Living in limbo is no way to live. The signs and actions were pretty straightforward. She made that decision and continued her walk with God. Even though things were not perfect, they weren't in limbo. She finally had a breath of fresh air and could completely heal. The work she started helped elevate her mentality. She saw the errors of her ways, especially in front of their children, and shifted. She was no longer stuck due to fear. She could see how fear gripped and kept her stagnant. She learned to stop talking from her emotions but from the things she desired. It was challenging because she made this a habit. Whatever Dennis didn't do had her on an emotional roller coaster. It took quite some time, but she broke those habits and changed her life for the better! Dennis learned later that his behavior was not beneficial to their children, and they suffered at the hands of his neglect. Again the same applies whether people have made mistakes in their past. Your past doesn't get to define you. You can turn things around if you do the work. Dennis's relationship with his children is on the mend now. It's all about changing your attitude, seeing things differently by coming from a place of love and understanding, and letting your mindset elevate you. Then grow, keep the faith and believe.

Being human, you're going to talk about your situation. However, it's time to elevate your mind by giving yourself a time limit. Give yourself three hours a day to discuss for 30 days. During that time, start your healing process. On day 31, spend two hours a day and give it all the attention it deserves. On Day 61, grant only one hour. Began to take back your life by concentrating on what you desire and not what's keeping you in bondage. Everyone's healing process is different, so adjust this accordingly. This guideline is for those ready to come out of the mental bondage their past has held them in. The past that is still wreaking havoc on your life! Get yourself into a rhythm of giving less energy to the situation and more power to the prosperity you rightfully deserve. It takes discipline and fighting your flesh versus your spirit. Supplying fuel to the good you desire certainly opens up more doors of good fortune to flow through! Creativity flows differently on a constant plane and not a roller coaster. You're not looking for another to make you happy, but they can add happiness to your life. You're not looking outward as much but looking inward and doing the work as you grow through different life phases. When you face challenges, you'll recall how God brought you through your last one and will build that trust in Him like never before. Will you be challenged with that previous statement. What do you think? The difference now is that you have a solid foundation to stand on, and it's no longer fear, hurt, guilt, shame, blame, bitterness, and unforgiveness. When your foundation is strong, your knees don't easily buckle anymore. Your thought process will be more of joy, laughter, happiness even when you're going through some challenges. You'll yearn to get back to that positive place. Understand that your faith will be tested. Weathering the storm won't look like it did in the past. God has brought you out of storms stay rooted and planted in Him continue to elevate, keep the faith, grow and believe.

Chapter 6

Elevate, Grow, Keep the Faith & Believe

If we, as people, don't take a long look at what we're going through and be candid with ourselves and others, history will repeat itself. Your mental well-being is fundamental to your spouse, children, family, friends, partners, coworkers, etc. They will either see you overcome and thrive or continue in a spiral downfall and succumb to your fears and anxiety. You could constantly look at others instead of taking accountability for your own life. But it's best to look inwardly, break free and then see how you can help others. I'm called to break generational curses for my family. Through God's grace, I'm doing just that. I'm navigating in waters that no one else in my family has. Sometimes it's lonely! People will think and feel how they want about you, but you have to stay the course. You can't detour or turn back because you've come too far. Your children need you to break these cycles so they won't have to deal with them. Instead of struggling with those curses, they can build more significant bridges for the family and the world at large. This is some of the benefits of

Changing your perspective to change what your life is about.

Elevate, grow, keep the faith, and believe as you navigate this passage of life by learning to get out of your emotions, for there's no intelligence in them. Don't be led by your feelings but be led by the Spirit. Place your trust in God and be steadfast and unmovable as you go through life's journey. If God told you, then believe Him! Stop trying to fight trouble in your own strength; instead, give it to God. Go through the transformation and get excited to meet the new you coming out of this. You have to trust the processor (God), so you can trust the process! Nothing grows, evolve, elevates nor keep the faith and believes without going through a process. Sheila had to lose her marital home, go through a separation and divorce, face single parenting and financial issues, along with other challenges, for God to develop her character. God revealed to her that she didn't lose, but she actually gained. She got to know herself even more by cultivating her relationship with Him. She acquired a more profound revelation about marriage too. A marriage is a union of two, but each individual has their own purposes and collective purpose. You complement and sharpen each other. You're each others' mirror of the area that God wants to work on. You have to be willing to progress and say, "God fix those areas in me as you fix those areas in my spouse."

Then be open to allow God to continue the work in both of you that's needed. You had to go through heartbreaks to stop connecting to everybody. You can't just allow anyone in your space. You're special and set apart by God. Therefore, it takes a unique man or woman to handle and support the anointing on your life. This growing process is preparing you to protect and govern the anointing on your mate. In knowing this understand you two are a team, not enemies.

Naomi had to change her perspective to forgive her mother and sister after discerning who the real enemy was. The enemy tried to break her at a young age because of how powerful a difference she'd make as an adult. God knew that she would healthily break the silence to help not only hers but others break free of their family's unhealed areas. Your spouse, sibling, parent, coworker, in-laws are not your enemy. It's the enemy behind the inner you using tactics and strategies to keep people in fear and mental bondage from their brokenness. When you break free of the mental bondage that has kept you paralyzed and step into living life with purpose, you become the vessel in the earth realm that God uses to bless people all over the world. You'll be the answer to prayers. As you learn more about God, you will learn more about your positions in life. More levels are revealed, and you won't look, think, feel, or behave as you did before. Popularity won't bother you because you're created to influence the multitudes God has predestined you to reach! Elevate your mind, grow, keep the faith and believe. Your journey is the path to birth what's inside of you! You have to walk this path to come out of your comfort zone. Your destiny and purpose will follow. God can use anything to realign you. Heard of growing pains? It's simply leaving the worries that held you captive behind to establish a rhythm of constant growth. Your commitments will shift. You're more selective of what you feed your mind and what absorbs your time and energy. Your circle of friends will adjust, and you'll invite positive vibes while letting go of drama. Some connections will be challenging to break; however, to get to a plateau you've never been to, you've got to do something you've never done before. Stay focused, purpose-driven, and ready to grow. God will open your eyes to acquaintances, friends, and family too. You'll adapt and love some people from a distance until they improve. Don't tell everyone what you're trying to accomplish. They can't relate to specific dreams because God gave you the vision, not them. You'll be directed to others in the field you're headed. It may seem intimidating but connect and be mentored. Don't seek to be the most knowledgeable person in your group. That's not growth. That's insecurity. You have to be open to learning and growing no matter where you start. Hone in on your goals.

Some people will have an issue with you advancing and say degrading things or try to make you feel guilty. Don't get bogged down with negative talk. Those tactics use to weigh you down but will soon roll off your back. They lied and talked about Jesus Christ. So stay focused, pray for them, and keep moving in the direction you're being led. God will open doors for you and close doors that are not beneficial too. Don't let challenges break you or have you stuck; instead, let them make you. Identify the inner strength that God placed inside of you. You were born to overcome adversity, challenges, heartaches, and pains. You were born to be a trend-setter. People may try to compete with you, but actually, they are inspired by you. It all depends on how you look at things. You are the inspiration people need to come out of their old ways and seek purpose.

Once I pursued life and happiness, I could hear God more clearly than just crying out in the midnight hour to make it through the night. I came out of mental bondages and started engaging in things that I'd put on hold for years. Spending more intentional time with God, my affirmations were specific, planning meals, working out regularly, creating more quality events with my children and family, revamping businesses, bringing vision into its proper place, and helping others. I went from sleeping on my bedroom floor to finally having a bedroom set in a few years. Every step was rebuilding. Every stride was developing my character. Building the spiritual muscles, I didn't realize I had. He was strengthening me to handle all the things I'm created to do. Everything that I'd encountered and experienced was all working to mold me into the woman God created me to be! I didn't lose; I gained stronger insight of my purpose, a deeper consciousness of me!

It's essential to step into whom God shaped and formed you to be, or else you'd be doing yourself and everyone connected to your purpose a disservice. Your life has meaning! Your words have power! So watch what you say, think, and feel. God is the 'Ultimate Navigator' of your life, and he'll lead you to the places he's called you! He knows which way you need to go. Who you need to connect with and who can no longer accompany you. When he removes people from your life, that's a mature moment. Lovingly, wish people the best and let them go. If not, you'll hinder your purpose and theirs too. So let go of trying to control everything, trying to have everything flow your way, go your way, when you want it, how you want it, and delivered in the package you wish to receive it in. Time to let go of all your pretenses. Accept that God's ways are not your ways and His thoughts are not your thoughts! Having a Christ-like mindset means surrendering your way, your will to His! No matter what challenges you go through, you must believe that God has your highest good in mind. That what he predestined you to do he will reroute you and get you back on course headed to your intended destination. What he's called you to do will make room and provision for you. Stay the course, trust, and believe that God got you covered and will never leave nor forsake you. The battle in your mind happens when you're not trusting God and still choose to do things your way. Change your attitude by selecting God's will instead of yours. Make a choice today surrender it all, every circumstance, fear, hurt, and pain so you can see things differently. Let your mindset take you to new altitudes as you shed off the old person and step into the New You! Elevate, grow, keep the Faith, and believe that you can change your perspective by changing your life through God. Break free of the mental bondages and live life with purpose.

Chapter 7

Change Your Perspective Process

Two Methods

1. Release Letter Method (Recommended)

2. Release Discussion Method by phone with a trusted 3rd party present for **(non-violent sit uat ions ONLY)**

*   ***Release Letter Method*** - write a letter about the situation. List what occurred, how it made you feel, and if it's still inflicting pain in your life. What can be done to resolve it? List the role you played (if applicable). What have you learned from this situation? Apologize and make peace within the letter. Release that baggage and all involved.

*   ***Release Discussion Method*** by Phone - when you have a phone discussion with a trusted 3rd party present, such as a therapist for **(non-violent situations ONLY).** You come to the conversation with a mindset of resolve, listen, take accountability, not refute, and make peace with what occurred. Document the date and time in the

journal section of this book. Follow the steps below.

- Depending on which method you use, say the applicable prayer from the 1st Chapter renouncing the effect and fear of this situation in your life. Ask God to uproot everything associated with the incident, consciously and subconsciously. Relinquish its power over your life. Then receive deliverance.

- Change your attitude; come from a place of love and understanding.

- Look at the situation differently. Don't look at it from a victim mentality but a victor. You made it through the problem, and you don't look like what you've been through. Change your perspective so that you're not so easily offended but extend love to others.

- This situation helped you grow. Take a deep look into how you've evolved. God can use anything to elevate your mindset. Choose to forgive and limit your chatter about the situation. Your words have power! You don't want to reap the words you sow. *Remember:* When going through challenges, don't say what you feel, which can bring about more damaging issues. Elevate and speak life.

This process helps you break out of old habits of giving

too much time and energy to non-productive entities:

- In your first 30 days, give yourself three hours only to discuss your circumstance.

- Now on day 31, decrease the time to two hours.

- Once you reach your 61st day, only devote one hour to it.

- During this time, begin to document goals to aim for and accomplish.

- Give God praise for what he has done, even if you're still going through challenges.

- Speak affirmations

- Pray

- Monitor what you feed your spirit, mind, and body.

- Flow in Positive vibrations

- Don't forget to trust Gods process

Chapter 8

Affirmations

I love God.

I love Myself.

I am an overcomer.

I am beautiful/handsome inside and out.

I am happy because I choose to be.

I am loving, kind, thoughtful, and caring.

I am understanding and use wisdom.

I flow in positive vibrations.

I protect my peace.

I forgive and move forward in love.

I am honest, faithful, and true.

I love people where they are on their journey and continue to wish and pray for God's highest good for their lives.

I am free to live the life I was created to live.

I am living life with purpose.

I am uniquely and wonderfully made.

I am successful and prosperous.

I love my journey of life, and It's getting more incredible each day.

I'm excited about my present and future.

I am creative and have a brilliant mind.

I make a difference in my family.

I make a difference in the world.

I am Healthy, Healed, and Whole.

I listen and speak from a place of love and understanding.

I know my journey is just for me.

I don't compare nor compete with anyone but myself.

I look at life from a hopeful perspective.

I change my perspective so that I can change my life for the better.

I speak life and not what I feel.

I'm excited to grow.

I trust the processor (God), and I trust His process.

Chapter 9

Prayer

Lord, I thank you for blessing me to overcome the battles in my mind, breaking free of the mental bondages, changing my attitude. I've chosen to see things differently and allow the altitude of my mindset to elevate me so I can grow in you. I'm keeping the faith and believing that you have delivered me from the things I have renounced. Those things have been uprooted, and they will no longer wreak havoc in my life. I live free of my past, and I'm stepping into all that you've called me to be. I'm getting out of my feelings! I refuse to walk around in unforgiveness. That situation or that person doesn't get to have control over my life. I live free to do and be all that you've called me to be. I trust you, Lord! That's why I can trust this process because your healing is everlasting. Help me put the processes in place to keep me from going back into what you've delivered me from. I choose to delete, block, unfollow, disconnect from those that will keep me talking about the situation that you've delivered me from. I've come out of that situation, and I'm not letting anyone send me back into it. Put a guard over my mouth. I choose to speak life! Not what I feel. I wish people the best and pray that they heal and grow in you. Lord, I need you to help me think pleasant thoughts and see greatness for my life. I neutralize anything that I've spoken, thought, or gave energy to that is not your will for my life. Help me learn and grow through my life journey to be a blessing for another. Help me realize that I'm not the only one and that my testimony helps free others from their past. Lord, thank you that my happiness, joy, strength, love, confidence is restored as I look to you to fill all the voids of the things that concern me. Thank you for being my way maker, provider, deliverer, healer, redeemer, miracle worker. Thank you for lighting my path so that my future gets brighter. I thank you that my life has turned around for the better. The blood of Jesus has cleansed me from all things, and I've come out as white as snow. I've been restored, and I can do all that you've told me I could do. You've qualified me, and that's enough! I am a child of the most high God. I've changed my perspective, which has changed my life for the better because of you, Lord. I thank you for being my protector, for keeping me, and for giving me a Christ-like mindset. I shall have healthy relationships and protect the peace that you've given me. I thank you for directing my steps. I hear you clearly, Lord, and I choose to obey. I have clarity and you've given me favor with people needed to carry out the vision you have for my life. I'm properly aligned and no weapon formed against me shall prosper, and every tongue which rises against me in judgment, you shall condemn. Isa 54:17 NKJV. I'm so grateful that you are always available to me and that your grace, mercy, and unconditional love have blessed me like never before. Greatness is my destiny. I am the head and not the tail, above and not beneath. I live and walk in divine order. I put on the whole armor of God, and I'm mindful of what I allow into my ear and eye gates. Thank you for working in my life, my spouse, children, family, friends, businesses, business partners, and jobs. (List all that you're thanking God for doing in your life). Everything that concerns me, you're in the midst of it working it out for my highest good! You're doing it for your glory. Thank you for being alpha and omega. The father that I can always depend on. Let your will be done in my life as I surrender everything to you. You know what's best and I trust you, Lord. I ask all these things in Jesus' Name I pray, Amen, Amen, and Amen.

Chapter 10

Journal

Keep notes of things you want to work on. Dates of letters written and situations released, prayers, affirmations, etc. This section is for you to use as you need.

_____

_____

_____

_____

_____

_____

_____

_____

_____

_____

_____

_____

_____

_____

_____

_____

_____

_____

_____

Thank You

I pray that this book helped encourage you to step into healing and let go of all that has held you captive. I wish you all the success that God has for you in Changing Your Perspective so that You can Change Your Life by breaking free of the mental bondages and living life with purpose!

Please be sure to leave a review on the platform that you've purchased this book from.

Kind Regards,

Charlotte Cain

$19.97

ISBN 978-1-7371081-0-8

51997>

9 781737 108108